LEFT-HANDED

LEFT-HANDED

POEMS

Jonathan Galassi

ALFRED A. KNOPF · NEW YORK
2012

THIS IS A BORZOI BOOK
PUBLISHED BY ALFRED A. KNOPF

www.aaknopf.com/poetry

Knopf, Borzoi Books, and the colophon are registered
trademarks of Random House, Inc.

Poems from this collection were originally published in the
following: "Ruins" in *The Daily Beast* (May 2011); "Young,"
"The Crossing," "Middle-aged," "Barn Owl Song," "Once,"
and "August" in *The Paris Review* (December 2011); and
"Thalictrum and Cimicifuga" in *The New Yorker* (January
2012).

Library of Congress Cataloging-in-Publication Data

Galassi, Jonathan.
    Left-handed : poems / Jonathan Galassi.
       p. cm.
    "This is a Borzoi Book."
    ISBN 978-0-307-95708-5 (alk. paper)
    I. Title.
    PS3557.A387L44 2011
    811'.54—dc23   2011033753

Jacket photograph by Amani Willett/Gallery Stock
Jacket design by Chip Kidd
Manufactured in the United States of America
First Edition

TO FREDERICK SEIDEL

saepe mecum

And I let the fish go.

CONTENTS

LEFT-HANDED

Envoi

Love, I'm weighing every word,
palming them, gauging
if their heft is right
to carry their message.

There's just one message:
love, which wants to be
selfless, serene,
is always and only

anything but:
needs to be noticed,
asks to be answered,
burns to be returned.

Love, when you weigh
these words yourself
as they flicker
on your inner screen,

be kind, be kind,
be kind to the small syllables
struggling upstream,
poor things terrified

that they'll expire
stranded in electronic sand,
crazy little things
whose one desire

is to strike home in you
before they die
and only if you say so
end in fire.

A CLEAN SLATE

A Clean Slate

The flash and funk of fall,
the foldedness and fatedness
and fetidness of it,
are happening again.
Sharp colors and deciduous ideas
come down on the lawn.
And what I want to know
is where does it go when it's gone,
the profusion, the snow
and commotion,
the fire and confusion?
Why did it happen this way
and what took you so long?
All this kerfuffle
over a simple election,
all this connivance for a few
years of getting things wrong,
this sitting and staring
for just a few words
not in optimum order,
so much for so little.

Take me: am I so unreasonable
with my fears and desires,
here in the late middle, waiting,
feeling the endings of others,
conceiving my own?
And the ongoing future upstairs:
how great it continues, how great
the cycle replays,

though it's us on the rack.
When you're angry you're right
for an hour or a day,
then a new wind sets in
to rewrite your perspective.
I want you to know me, yes,
and I want to be right.
I want health
and truth in investment,
protection and courage
and comfort and power,
hour after hour
year after year after year.

Wintergreen, like ivy on the wall,
pretending it's not really dead, until
the fresh red leaves push the old ones aside.
Or hemlock, almost black against the snow,
a kind of life, and fragrant when it's crushed,
but not the sodden lyrical despairing
yellow-green of spring. And rain again:
fainter and fainter, over and over,
again and again,
and, yes, my hearing's fading,
the way the sense of smell went.
And the repetition's terrifying.
I want spring to come because
I want upheaval, flooding,
the excitement of the primal rite;
and I don't want spring to come
because it means another, one less spring.

Oceanic, hecticness
that might be exaltation
or despair

panic
under the undulant
spread of the hills
underworld
that opens in a word.

Half of me wants to surrender
to nothingness
to terror
the other's all
heroic order and command
always the seesaw back-and-forth
always the lack of the great here and now.

Who remembers
                    Delayed Gratification?
Save it for later,
for a rainy day.
But later's now,
late's now.
Taste while you can,
forget tomorrow.
Think when tomorrow comes.
Mortgage the future.

Tell me, can there ever be enough
time to weed the driveway and edit the woods,
or try the potentilla in that difficult corner?
Are there ever enough days like this one,
sunny and still, held close before the turn?
The lady seems to think so,
sleeping the rich brown summer away
on her stolid cenotaph in the Borghese gardens,
guarded by English deer and English trees.
She seems a bit uncomfortable on her stone pillow
while her not-so-callipygian companion
keeps an eye out for barbarians
from a nearby pillar. And you're sleeping
too as I write this. But not a sleep of stone;
no: something warm and undulant,
something to breathe with and burrow into.

I wanted to give you a picture
of how it works,
the way the wave of dissolution
rises out of desire
and rides me home

and how the other's open
tenderness and need
are always driving the bus
how little I feel able
to wear the clothes that are laid out on the bed
how I admire those who wouldn't wear them
how I lack the courage not to wear them.
But that's not the whole story:
I like wearing them;
I like being a man
when I can.

Other apparition, avatar
I still see you, we have come this far.
I still know you, you still don't know me.
I'm still looking—what is there to see?
Nothing echoes from the far
spaces where you say you are,
no infusing the intense palette
with local color and ejaculate,
hunger coming clean again
falling in the winter rain.
Other apparition, avatar
though you're very far I feel you here

*

but never together

*

When the intertextual metamorphic
pain that was passion
reads back as faint and slow and ashen
and interiority gets turned out like a sleeve
look to find me in the cleansing wind
off the teahouse underneath the hill.
You never knew me and you never will.

Young

I tried, and each attempt was a fiasco.
I yearned, but every love of mine was wrong.
I needed, and the shame was overwhelming.
I failed, and so I hated being young.

Still Life

Somewhere you're always twenty-four
and lie on sand
so hot you have to stand still
before you can move.
It's early but your tan is Arab-dark,
your hair incongruous blond.

A body rich in possibilities
like any body: you had longish hands
and wide eyes, blurred by something
you had to reach to feel.
Part liquor, part intelligence,
it might have been real.

At the little lake you knew about
we were silent
while the bloodred sun
rang down on the scenic view:
white barns and a tree or two
in the flyblown water.

We could have cracked
its mirror with a rock,
a branch that might have lifted
something muddy to the surface.
Instead we kept on staring
and the sun set, several times.

Somewhere it keeps setting,
waits for one of us to still
the thread that hums between us,
not gossamer but steel.

Somewhere you shimmer like the lake,
the picture on the glass is real,
and one of us says what we didn't say,
feels what we didn't feel.

The Room on Naxos

In that room on Naxos,
the hotel room in the
little one-street har-
bor town we walked a
mile or two from to
the perfect mile-long
beach with only a few
Germans Gerhard and
Ulrike and the wiz-
ened woman archeolo-
gist with her much
younger lover and
that sweet taverna
just for us the daz-
zling beach where we
swam nude and where
I tried to lift you
out of the water like
a goddess doing beau-
tifully until the wa-
ter wasn't under you
—in that lamplit bed-
room (or was it on the
ferry was it later?)
when I tried to tell
you it had been won-
derful but it was
over you didn't hear
me didn't understand
what I was saying and

I kept on going so as
not to hurt you and
then fell in love a-
gain: Where would we
be now if you had
heard me if our is-
land time had been a
sun-dazed moment not
the prelude to a long
long story rife with
declarations and ad-
missions one or the
other of us didn't
hear?

Reconstructed Poem

Tonight the city lights are wild;
they burn the oscillating air.
Their flickering is all that moves,
soundless, dense, and pure.

This could be a view of hell
approaching from the south:
a mile-long double row of flares
banked at its mouth.

You too are silent and your look
is elsewhere, no return, no spark.
Ahead of us a cigarette
falls in the dark,

breaks into little flakes of fire,
heightens the native sense of sin.
I am as far from my desire
as I have ever been.

Shine

Riches, a little dollop of your shine
is everything I need to make my day:
cheek of polished apple, wink of wine,
forehead semaphore along my way;
or torque of body gilded in the spray,
toothy, tonguey, stretched-saliva grin,
melon water sliding off a chin,
eyelash droplet where a sunbeam plays.
Slick of foam that glistens on the rim,
coffee cream curl, baby oil spill, oh,
and gabardine lap-luster, zipper shimmer,
moiré patent-leather afterglow:
I hoard it, all the gold that makes you mine
(like finger ink spot, gaudy brilliantine).

Rootwork

The way a blade
of grass hides
in plain sight
in the border as
if it belonged
I hide in life.

*

Clearing brush
is very salutary:
good for the
woods, good for
the heart and
soul. But there
are thickets
that we can't
untangle. We can
only stare at how
the bittersweet
murders the
laurel by the lake.
Tear it down, rip
it out: it's back
next year just as
rapacious.

*

I try to get at
the yellow root
of the barberry
that threatens to
overwhelm my
woods. The prickly
lobe-leaved
branches that fan
out in all direc-
tions aren't the
problem. It's the
roots that are
now and forever.

*

And Roundup won't
eradicate the sim-
plest allium in
the terrace crev-
ice, either. Eter-
nal return . . . and
your root world
and mine? Sister,
don't even bother.

Thalictrum and Cimicifuga

Thalictrum and Cimicifuga,
married for life:
"I love your filigreed purply curls."
"I love your pompous white spikes."

Look at them swaying out in the wind,
bowed by the nastiest weather:
always reverting to genus
and always together.

The Last Swim of Summer

ought to be swum
without knowing it,
afternoon lost to
re-finding the rock
you can stand on
way out past the
raft, the flat one
that lines up four-
square with the door
of the boathouse.

Freestyle and back-
stroke and hours on
the dock nattering
on while the low sun
keeps setting fin-
gers and toes getting
number and number . . .
how could we know
we were swimming the
last swim of summer?*

*It wasn't actually—that came weeks after, it was so warm that fall.

Ours

This house these walls were ours
and everything inside them the
lawns the trees the flower beds
the stone walls not the fern
walk that is Alison's but it's the
way the first light filters
through the thinned-out branch-
es part of us the ancient
apple orchard the hydrangeas
yellowed lily leaves the old
barn the new studio that you and
Chris created for me and the ice-
house and the light is ours the
angled brilliance and the funk of
fall the weather's turned the
snow the stairs the stars out on
the lawn the cold coyotes' calls
are ours the view from the mar-
tini bench the copper beech the
thyme terrace and the new one
and the girls are ours the young
shad and the lilacs and our
square bed and the birch room
and the teahouse sunset apple
smoke the flame azaleas that
didn't take the peonies the si-
lences and evening unraveling
the immense white pine and fuel
oil smell were ours these rooms

are ours the pictures sofas car-
pets my grandmother's bud vase
the coin silver spoons and Eloise
is ours and Phoebe was this room
is ours the square bed and the
threshing here was ours the si-
lences the Paris bedspread and
the dressers and my red desk in
the alcove and your bathroom tub
the inky tentacles e-mail was ours
and phone calls and what makes
you think you're you was always
ours

     pretend you're with me as
you read this all the empty
hours were ours the rattling down
the hall the perfect view across
the road the hills the walls the
white fence fallen branches bit-
tersweet the stairs the girls are
ours the love the friends the
silences your voice your eyes your
hair your neck the beauty all are
ours the empty mornings and the
silences were ours the staring at
the fire before it died the grappa
and the whiskey in etched glasses
and the bellows the black marble
fireplace and Chris's gavel Mol-
lie's picture Christopher's two
drawings dinner by the fire was
ours the sausages the peppermint

foot rub your cowhide slippers
endless books too many you kept
saying in the halfway house hu-
midity and hummingbirds all ours
all ours the afternoons the misty
mornings looking up the lawn the
copper beech the peegees turning
purple Haystack and the deep
sleeps the Bald Mountain treks
the fern walk and the two chairs
by the stream we never sat in
and the little living room and
Libby's paths the Alfords' rugs the
girls my parents' nesting tables
Pete Street's hidden staircase
all the evenings the talk the
laughter all the music all the
friends the silences the girls and
everything that was and wasn't
ours

and hours were ours the
walks the silent drives the si-
lences unspoken love the lacks
the guilt the missing the alone-
ness what we couldn't do the
what we didn't say the things I
couldn't do the one I couldn't
be and wanted to and didn't is
ours too and rage is ours and
loss and hours alone are ours
the silences the hall the girls
and the unknown was ours the fu-
ture that we couldn't share the

fear the falling leaves and fail-
ing ruining the fault lines and
the love lines and incomprehen-
sion and the need to know and to
be known and broken faith deri-
sion denigration power was ours
and powerlessness and struggle
and my twisted heart that got un-
twisted and your face your voice
your neck your back the tears
the girls the life I left the lost
life all of it was ours is ours
was ours is ours was

THE CROSSING

The Crossing

When cloud cover com-
plicates the crossing
all we can do is look
out into dawn its wild
striations fiery or
sullied by smoke and
tell ourselves that
we'll get back to
where we would have
been if accidents or
operations hadn't in-
tervened. You were
just over fortunate
fragile frequent
flexible flyer; you
floated till you fal-
tered in ways I don't
understand. I'm an
intruder, I don't
speak for you, who
knows if you hear me.
But time runs on for
you too, your back-
ward glance is just
like mine, and if I
imitate your sleep-
lessness it's out of
influence or em-
pathy.

Yes, winning
matters in the upper
world, and you
worship it with your
deals and fabulous
plans. What speaks to
me is something more
intensive: the glass
that's never full,
commotion, energy—
a stand. I won't say
more, I with no
rights in the matter.
But do this sometime
now you're open: look
while you're leaping,
look, and look again.
Let unshed tears re-
deem the eyes that
have seen what
they've seen.

O Youth and Beauty

Your e-mail said that Cambridge was awash
in gilded youth that weekend, gathering
to "get fuzzy" for the Head of the Charles.
"Heartbreaking," you added, and I had to smile.
"Spooky to see so many pink-faced kids
glazing along the banks, then piling
too many into cars and racing off
to heighten their states." Heartbreaking
knowing that they spoke to you,
going to a party you weren't part of.

A little early for nostalgia?
It never is, I know, but why the pangs?
That they could be so ravishing and clueless,
squandering their moment (but they have to,
isn't that what makes them glow?).
Or was it that it's someone else's turn,
that you're no longer quite so lost and free,
sober, hitched, responsible,
with just the first shadings of age?
That's nothing: let me tell you, boy.
Enjoy the late spring, it's the mildest weather,
Bask in your sunstruck run-up to noon.
                                    As for the party,

it's on there in the boathouse
where the band is playing standards
that no one in my generation or yours
ever danced to but at weddings.
You can swim the water if you want to.
It's flowing past your summer window,

bearing its reliable supply
of youth and beauty.
Look, they're leaning out
in tees and cords and goose bumps,
as the fragile, tensile shells plow on.
That's you in the front row,
"shouting, amazed" at the finish line,
happy to be cold and hoarse
and swaying with the crowd
the whole gunmetal afternoon,
all of you chanting in a broken descant
then wandering off to dinner and each other,
part of the party, before it moved on.

Our Landscape Is Hills

Why do I end up consoled
by you whom I want to console,
whose reticence is more telling
than all my complaining?
And how did you get to be older,
ancient of days? What I want
is to know every slightest thing
that did and didn't happen,
and afterwards to let go
of every loss,
every hurt,
and look to the future.

Our landscape is hills called mountains,
hills "like a rack of dishes"
cut by another river,
and I crossed to your side long ago.
The trees seem taller here,
heroic, elegiac,
but that could be faulty memory
or anesthesia.
Our landscape is hills, and our time
is the no-man's-land of twilight,
the half-light of dawn coming on,
when shapes lose definition
and joy and grief are one.

What I know is I want
to walk these trails with you,
to fish with you in the river

whose catch you have to throw back.
I want you to understand
how much you owe to the hills
and the water falling there.
I want you one with the air,
the spring chill, and the mist.
If I could give you this
I would have done my part.

Another Arrival

[lost]

. . .
I know you know
what remorse is like, friend.
I know you know
how it feels to have faltered.
All I can add
is the convict's old saw:

Honest, Your Honor,
it's not what I meant.
Here in my heart
it was all innocent.

Here in my heart
I'm still strong and reliable,
upright and viable,
sunstruck and sure.

Glass

That glare in the
grass is the last
bit of glass from
the window that
fell in a wild
winter wind. I've
spent the morning
trying to rake up
the wreckage. The
terrace is clear
now the pooled
thyme's about to
go green. Imagine
the blast that
could rip the old
storm off its
hinges and hurl
it down onto the
bench sending sliv-
ers and splinters
every which way.
It might have
been just a gust
that rode over
sailing along on
its everyday path
of destruction.
But it's hard to
believe that here
down on all fours

working to pry
little numberless
pieces out of
the crevices feel-
ing my crablike
way on the
obdurate stones.

A Wave

eleven stories up
and you're off
bounding as al-
ways on the balls
of your feet mak-
ing the crossing
into your Tenth
Street life to
find your band of
instant comrades
sworn in fealty
against a common
foe that huge
half-hidden world
of yours I'll
never know.

Hearing you it's
hard to recognize
that you could be
adept at dissolu-
tion. To me your
husky tones meant
loving-kindness,
upland acceptance,
rooms without
shame. Please, no
more visits to
the underworld.
We need you here

if we're not to
be phantoms our-
selves. I'm still
hollow, half-de-
stroyed, scooped
out by guilt, by
grief from watch-
ing you fold,
from losing my
way. But I don't
have your grit,
your steel, your
skill at hiding
despair. It comes,
it's cold and
simple and it's
here. So hail and
farewell, bad boy,
older brother, prod-
igal son I'll never
have. Thrive,
stride in your
new life, learn
to be glad. More
of me than I know
goes with you in-
to your bright-
eyed biddable
future. More of
you is staying
with me, flowing
from the current
of your jaunty
benediction.

The Halt and the Lame

I'll tell you what the
meaning of is, is: it's
gratitude to be upright
sweatslicked and tee-
tering tilted tectonic
sidewalk slab fetor of
garbage weeds in the
empty cracked parking
lot choking the old
rhododendron.

Out with my brothers
and sisters the halt
and the lame dragging
a gimp leg and loving
the pain loving the
trouble it takes to
recover the exquisite
game plan to get there
from here while the
cartilage grinds in the
lovely grim city stunt-
ed trees going cold
turkey in fried ozone
out with my brothers
and sisters the halt and
the lame.

The Pool Was Full

The pool was full for
once this afternoon.
The trees were
drenched in lateness
too, everything back-
lit, tempered, gor-
geous: things as they
ought to be and never
are.
    The new trail
runs along the brook,
carved out of bar-
berry and honeysuck-
le. This time of year
the water's just a
trickle, yet somehow
the pool was full:
a hidden source must
keep its water level
while it rests here
on its journey south
before it reaches
the devouring mouth
of the river, and
then on—the way our
little life is up
and gone.
        Just now,
though, crows were
strutting on the lawn,

cicadas beat their un-
relenting beat, the
phlox held still, un-
troubled by a breeze.
For once the world
relaxed its pull, the
empty afternoon un-
knit in ease. The
brook's a trickle
but the pool was full.

Apples and Oranges

Apples are not the
only fruit. Yes,
they hang out in
the open up in the
branches, stealing
the sun to return
it in burgeoning
flavor. Oranges
ripen in groves or
in orangeries,
growing the thick
hides that cover
their segmented
sweetness, their
vitamin riches,
their tartness
and fizz.

Friends, my bowl
has been filled
with a high hill
of oranges. Fruit
of all kinds from
Seville and Valen-
cia, Florida, Jaffa:
temples and navels,
blood oranges, man-
darins. Now the
light's changing
they all of a sud-

den are here for
the taking, an or-
ange a day.
       Come
share my oranges,
all shapes and siz-
es and orangey col-
ors: some are as
gold as the sun it-
self; some are un-
dyed, so green
they might almost
be apples.

The Shorter Days

are back—dry
leaves and dark
by seven, up at
seven in the
dark: just the
way it was a
year ago. But
what I was a
year ago I'm
not.

The world
is darker:
nights take
longer, fre-
quent travel-
ers no longer
fly. They take
meetings but
avoid hotels.
Eyes redeemed,
lives righted,
soon they'll
look to the fu-
ture.

Which is
as it should
be, and we're
grateful.

Pray for them,
cheer them as
they cycle by.
Try to cherish
every shorter
day. Be rich:
you know the
year will soon
be old. (But
where to bury
my unwanted
gold?)

Barn Owl Song

If a man is his desire
if a man is his desire
if a man is his desire
who cooks for you?

If a man has been on fire
if a man has been on fire
I say, if a man has been on fire
who cooks for you?
Who cooks for you?

If a man has walked a wire
if a man has walked a wire
I say
if a man has walked a wire
will it lead to his desire
was it why he was on fire?
Tell me what's true
and
who cooks for you
who cooks for you
who
who
who cooks for you?

If a man has been a liar
if a man has been a liar
I say, if a man has been a liar
was it that he was on fire
did he misconstrue desire?

Tell me what's true
and
who cooks for you
who
who
who
who cooks for you

If a man has worn a wire
if a man has worn a wire
I say
if a man has worn a wire
passing through the hardest fire
that was burning his desire
can he stay up on the wire
does it mean he is a liar?
Tell me what's true
and
who cooks for you
who
who
who cooks for you?

BlackBerry Poems

If

I could lie there
next to you wide-
eyed while the
stars pressed
down their fatal
weight imprint-
ing us with his-
tories and fu-
tures as their
laser light tat-
tooed us with ex-
perience; if I
could feel your
nightly prayers
radiating in your
pulse bringing
both remorse and
consolation; I'd
rise and go the
marked man that
I am biolumi-
nescent with
enough happiness
to last me through
my days grandiose
with gratitude
and praise.

Water

My brother our love
is an underground
river fast and full
under the map of a
changeable land. It
can be harsh unfor-
giving no matter: a
drinkable swimmable
tight-braided rope
of invisible water
is moving there
depthless and si-
lent and mineral
pouring through
limestone ahead in-
to sinuous life.
You hear what I'm
feeling I feel what
you live through we
see what we've seen;
we bicker and hope
and look backward
we weep and are
glad. Affinity
flows down a line
that is static with
laughter. Others
may see you as
earth or as fire as

air or as absence
as nightfall or
later; my brother,
to me it's been
given to know you
as water.

Hope has a voice—it's
what I heard in you:
the rumble of rebirth,
the yawp of rage, the
same impertinent un-
settling new sound
that both of us want
on the page and almost
never find; but some-
one comes into a room
and things change
suddenly. You can hear
hope in how a tensed
wire thrums, in branch-
es cracking, breaking,
breaking free, saying a
man can change, can
tame his weather, set
his house in order,
true his tone. These
lines are voicing hope
for you, my brother, for
your fierce life and
for my struggling own
. . . (And then there is
the hope that you might
be alive in this the
way you are in me.)

A Little Tour Around Your Room

Start with the view, the late,
great Empire State Building
soldiering solo in your north-
facing windows with the rough-
diamond city spread-eagled be-
low: how New York is that?
And your stolen Sharon road
sign and Empire State Build-
ing model (a present from
Philip?) your grandfather's
insulators on the sill and
photos of eerie faces and un-
settled scenery. Here's your
collection of caps and your
terrace with its tufted prai-
rie grass your little couch
and table and piles of papers
—surely enough reading for a
lifetime. And here's Benny
mewing looking for you like
me and your aged Italian
leather chair that's missing
a button and the garden table
with its pair of folding seats
I bet you never eat at and
your TV on its stable stand
of books, so many books (I
love that the computer's in
the kitchen). And here's your
closet with your cache of se-

crets, your strong box
stuffed with histories and
letters, your scarves and
jeans and scuffed shoes and
"Not A Supplicant" T-shirts,
enough for a team. Here are
the piles of the poetry that
stings you and your music,
your BlackBerry and the
phone you can't survive with-
out and often lose, your Fer-
ragamo coat and mittens and
wallet and keys and bag.
Here's Noah's shirt and the
golden bed—where are you?

Middle-aged

He was middle-aged which
means that the mixture of
death and life in him was
still undetermined. And
all of a sudden he took
an unwarranted turn—im-
pulsive, convulsive. As
in those nineteenth-cen-
tury plays where the
roof gets blown off the
conventional house and
the audience is left to
gape at the bare-headed
heroine—him. He has a
gift for self-serious hy-
perbole and he resorts
to it regularly to de-
scribe and explain his
behavior. Not that any-
thing happened. But he
stared into something, an
abyss or a garden, and
now in the aftermath he's
more alone than before.
He has not been forgiven,
not that he wants to be.
What he wants is to know
what he saw, that it was-
n't theatrics. But that's

hard to achieve, things
being what they are, the
others implicated being
themselves. So he walks
in circles and wonders
and kicks at the leaves.

The Scarf

When or if you wear
your Loro Piana scarf
the one I gave you
once upon a time why
does it have to sit so
heavy on your shoul-
ders? I don't know
how my dream became
a contraption for un-
happiness a red flag
a noose when it was
engendered by joy.
What I want today is
to sit with you in
the sun to watch the
parade and critique
the bands marching
by. I wish you could
wear my scarf as
lightly as Julia's. I
wish my step were as
sharp my feeling as
simple my own shoul-
ders free of the bur-
den that bends them
like lead.

The New Life

Jude, the new life
starts today; time
to put your jacket
on. Time to put
the past away and
venture out of
hurt and stress
into courage, calm,
and tenderness.
When sun or lamp-
light hits your
desk, or, better,
when the city sky
is gray with rain,
no tree in sight,
or it is night, I
hope this book of
brass will shine
(it needs some
polish now and
then) telling you
who are so dear to
me, that I am al-
ways, always near.

Night Letter

Spring night: down below the
roads are dewy ribbons curl-
ing through black-and-silver
woods: a lunar landscape,
but the moon is with us,
little fingernail cocooned
in mist, bright stamp on
the letter of night.

Spring ferment oozing from
the still-cold ground. I
could hear peepers if this
window opened under our
moon—it's shining for you
too over the city, though
it's hidden. Our sky: the
rain is falling where you
are, as gently and relent-
lessly as here . . . but other-
wise it's hard to guess what
we share now—something ten-
uous and undefined, maybe a
glint, an SOS—but nothing's
clear in this sodden half-
light where time flattens
what we feel. . . .

                I can't
write you anymore. It's not
that I don't have too much

to say, but there's no echo
and my words trail off;
they're old, like breath gone
stale. I can let go of this,
I even want to; it's just
that something lived in me
for a time and was tremen-
dous and made terrible de-
mands; and there's an after-
shock, a residue. I wanted
more. I do. I always will.

Now I hope you'll break out
and make off with the prize,
which is mutual love. I took
my chance; I earned my
stripes; if peace can seem
like a stage of emptiness, I
can still believe I'll be
rich in another sun, maybe
the new one starting to suc-
ceed this hushed night with
its flat shadows and wet
roads—the realm of your un-
bending gentleness that
helped me extinguish my
dream.

Second Night Letter

[lost]

Seventh Avenue

I own myself today and this
wise old road owns itself too
raveling out of the park
then straightening as it
rolls past the caviar palace
the gingerbread Alwyn Court
and scrofulous Osborne and
the white-and-gold hall where
unearthly music makes itself
heard then Carnegie Deli your
corner and louder crowded
more gritty delights as we
trundle down to the Square
that isn't a square but a di-
gital funnel a neon-lit hour-
glass the mind-bending rau-
cous strobe eye of the cyber-
space needle with crawling
news stock prices underwear
sex and destruction we meet
and we greet one careering
path crosses another or else
we travel in sync for awhile
until someone peels off
that's the way of the world
and there's nothing to hide
the hard truth not a single
real tree the whole trip down
this wide way that is yours
for me now though today I'm

along for the ride just the
peerless relentless sun print-
ing the sky and the tall
buildings' shade that was no
help at all in the punishing
cold when old Janus whipped
in from the Plains heading
somewhere remember? and on
through the desolate shallows
of flat Fashion Avenue
there's fading Macy's and
here comes Penn Station the
Garden's packed slow lonely
Brownian mingling kids in on
the look-out for something
but really afraid to engage
with our friends the love-sell-
ers and buyers the givers and
takers who reach out and touch
what I never could do and the
hawkers too hawking oblivion I
think I could use some of that
of an evening but you have
to come back or else not I
guess not if you can't or
don't want to I thank the God
I'm so uncomfortable with
every day that you did that
you chose to and here you are
living your spanking new life
as glad as a clam my dashing
bold ravenous tender bright
shrink-wrapped absorbent
fresh comrade and now we're

in Chelsea and here's good
old Barneys it's a museum now
Buddhist art isn't it Wil-
liams-Sonoma and here is your
sweet bleak home corner your
coffee shop up there's your
terrace from which you can
watch while the sky puts her
clothes on and takes them off
over and over entrancing the
ziggurat city those are your
windows so often pitch-dark
this is where you get off but
the highway keeps flowing
will take me on down to the
Village and then I'll become
someone else don't leave your
messenger bag crammed with
the hopes that you know how
to alchemize into plausible
song don't leave your cell
phone your line to your le-
gion of mothers and brothers
and sisters and hankering
swains this is your world
that I gape at in wonder and
fail to keep up with this is
your love nest your eagle's
nest home to your cockled
wounded yearning burning ever-
fending intractable heart
here's where you own yourself
Jude what we own is ourselves
not each other my knife and

enigma my much-adored out-
of-reach father and son we own
ourselves yes true we own our-
selves we own ourselves we own
ourselves we own ourselves
we're alone and we own
ourselves

Pretzels

You twisted your-
self into a pretzel
trying to tolerate
something you hated
in me it turned out
was essential. Does
that mean I should
twist myself into a
pretzel trying not
to be the thing that
made you twist
yourself into a
pretzel? Having
been salty and
wrenched for so
long it's a relief I
find to unwind and
simply be bent but
not twisted; neither
of us can be pret-
zels anymore. Why
is that so hard to
understand? I'm sad
about it too but
I'm not angry. No,
I'm glad I'm not
twisted into a pret-
zel. You be glad too.

Judgment

You talk about my
bad judgment as
if I had any.

Once

the train has left the
station you can't take it.
Once the promise has been
broke you can't unbreak it.

If the letter has been sent
you can't rewrite it.
If the cigarette's been smoked
you can't not light it.

Now the candle's snuffed
you can't see by it.
Once the seat's been sold
no one can buy it.

The phone is disconnected:
don't talk to it.
The window's painted black;
you won't see through it.

The Scotch tape end is lost,
you can't unwind it.
The earring's in the lake;
you'll never find it.

And now the money's squandered—
you can't give it
back. And time is short;
you have to live it.

Radical Hope

Darling, I'm running
on radical hope:
that the clouds will dispel
and our way will come clear,
that the UPS package
contains our relief,
that magic will bring us
an end to our grief.

But the signs at the crossroads
are pointing both ways
and the roundabout traffic
has no right-of-way.
It snakes through the town,
up the hill and back down,
and all of our pigeons
are coming to ground.

Where are the objects
of all my affections?
Will what I'm doing
result in right action?
The landslide has happened,
the bridge is unsound;
there's no backing up now,
no turning around.

So much for direction,
for learning and knowing,
for seeking and heeding,
for staying or going.
These were the ways
of the life that we've known
and all of this time
I've been going alone

and I can't anymore.
Will it happen this way?
Do you hear what I'm telling
you, softly, today?
Can you listen to me?
Are you right? Am I wrong?
The answer is somewhere
inside of this song.

The River

Can you see the river from
your window if you lean out
can you glimpse that patch
between the buildings gray
field of commingling muscle
traveling inexorable some-
where anywhere who knows
where pulling everything
along with it? Remember
your first dive in the elec-
tric chill at the brown
curve that rims the hills
and coolly navigates the
islands herons nest in past
the loosestrife banks and
you were ladled over un-
expected falls whitewater
surfing in the boulders to
emerge battered but exhila-
rated? Here the current's
more complacent stolid with
unchallenged power there's
no resisting but it was dif-
ferent there and then deeps
dangerous shallows choppy
unreliable more beautiful
perhaps but treacherous
alien until you learned to
swim inside it put its mantle
on its flow became your own

it brought you here. Now you
hardly notice when you sun
on the pier you don't hear
its sullen roar or catch
it flashing livid at dusk or
see the others flailing in
the wake . . . you may never
mouth it never cross its
bridges again but it does-
n't matter now you are the
river

BlackBerry Poems

Little Blue T-Shirt

floating on the court
at sunset little dis-
embodied sky-blue
T-shirt lifting in the
wind that sends it
chasing the imagined
bouncing ball: strain-
ing forward to return
the net serve arching
back for the lob
that's out of bounds
twisting heaving
half-moons at the
armpits little dark-
er diamond at the
sternum back stuck
to the torso that's
not there—
          little
blue T-shirt filled
out with the heaving
of the one who owns
it the triumphant
open heart exulting
hyperventilating
weeping little los-
ing winning sky-blue
T-shirt rising div-
ing flailing in the
wind

You Want What You Want

[lost]

and you get it,
one way or another . . .

Engine

of unhappiness, taker, bad
seed—why am I helpless
when I see you pass or hear
the gravel in your voice?

The Call

Waiting for the call
I do not want that I
solicited desire and
fear because it ties
me tighter to my
stake my love and
pain I hurry to at
every opportunity
waiting living while
I drink my coffee
scan the paper work
this poem little
phone beside me
little lifeline to my
love and pain with
its illuminated log
of all the many
calls recording just
how long they were
or weren't who initi-
ated them and almost
why waiting for the
call that will not
come hoping it won't
come and waiting
waiting

Our Dark Places

They are many:
silences trans-
actions mot-
tled love and
lack of love
envy cruelty
posturing with-
holding taunt-
ing all the
stuff of half-
love what is
spoiled what's
tainted meat
what isn't
free what has
a price tag
what lies un-
derneath what
isn't said
what doesn't
get enacted
our powers
our porno-
graphies with-
holding taint-
ed meat what
isn't said
what isn't
free what
lies beneath

Jude

The glow-fog of Christ-
minster from the hill-
top turned his head
but down in Marygreen
the village where he
had his outer being
brighter lights kept
him from being seen.
And even when he'd
learned the texts by
heart he found that
there was still no
entry into the spired
city under the arches
he had carved, because
there is no law of
transmutation. And
there were other fires
that dimmed or flared
and acted to exclude
our gentle Jude.

Jude, you're always
wanting a way in. Up
here the sun burns at
the ferns and future
asters and the half-
cut field rises behind
to make the fight feel
distant for an instant

but you keep scything
flailing endless gaping
El Dorado revving gyro-
scope of need shapely
vessel chipped and
scarred with living
ever avid to be filled
leaking inner light and
running late. Gentle
Jude my lovely Jude my
heartfelt heartworn
heartsick
heartless
Jude.

Independence Day

It's not what I want
to observe how you
light up a table or
clock your exploits
with one tremulous
boy or another but
it is what I'm able
to take in today
hustling behind as
you stride down
your own rocky
road little brother
cocky unsure ragged
bundle of selves in
a savory package
chasing your spec-
ters of beauty and
youth and bemused
at the wreckage.

It's not what I
want to hang in
with your pals
while the long
light outside makes
a show as it squan-
ders and rolls but
it is what it is
Jude the best we
can be given our

heads and our
hearts and our
disparate souls.
It's a wonderful
thing to behold from
the car seat to have
our day lose our way
be what we can and
we can't yes and
know you from way
over here—but it's
not what I want.

August

This world so
golden so un-
reachable this
August morning
with its hills
its tawny stub-
ble fields its
full-crowned
trees its sin-
gle scarlet
branches arch-
ing overhead
as desperate
music pours
from the
speakers is
reason enough
to live almost
although it's
hard acknowl-
edging that this
is what it
gives us: sim-
ple being
depthless mir-
rored imma-
nence daylong

and here for
the taking.

I want the
world to an-
swer back the
way the song
wants—shared
joy and shared
grief shared
adoration
spilling into
the unrepen-
tant void. And
today it al-
most does: sun-
struck seren-
ity and self-
content im-
mense impervi-
ous beauty
distant pres-
ent godly evi-
dence—as in
the near far
hills the
first most
gaudy leaves
the rough down
gold or russet
no hint of
gray yet on
your untouch-
able cheek.

I CAN SLEEP LATER

Breakfast

on my little terrace
shaded by my little tree of life.
Early morning summer haze,
coffee after swimming,
cherries, toast.
Time to plant some,
read some, dream some,
time to regret,
to mourn, desire.
Time to be up and about,
friends. I can sleep later.

His Letter on the Table

Hi, Hon.

I received your messages, but don't know if I should call. And if I called, what would I say? What could I say? It was only a short time ago I told you, "I love you," called you "Chicken Honey," and slapped you on your butt.

Those words of finality, they were so sudden and cut through us as though there was nothing left.

Yesterday, after you left for California, I came across your orange striped shirt hanging in the closet, sleeves rolled up, still fresh from wear, fresh with your scent. I took orange shirt off the bar and rested my face against it—orange shirt caressed my cheek; orange shirt cradled my soul; orange shirt took me back to our moments together:

the first time we met you grilled me and then took me home and introduced me to your friends;

lying naked in bed with you, as you gazed into my eyes and serenaded in a quivering voice, "I've got a crush on you," sending me peacefully adrift to sleep;

watching you snore in the movie theater, creating a disturbance, and then walking home—head down, back bent, your body slightly crouched—I drowned in emotion: "This is my hon."

Loving you, I love all four corners of you.

But the cut is too deep. Hon, I tried to hold on, but you were already gone. Please take care of yourself. I love you.

me

Left-handed

My parents understood I was left-handed
and didn't make me write against the grain
the way so many people their age had to.
Still, the western witch
barred the gate to the castle
where the enchanted chocolate cake
lay hidden: gooey, luscious,
pitch-black devil's food with butter icing.
The cake went stale;
I never got to kiss it into life
and be Prince Charming
with a sheepish butter-and-sugar face.
And I got stale too
till you came along, cupcake,
and everything turned midnight satin.

Could my story have been otherwise?
If the drawbridge had been down
could a bright knight
have led me on a different crusade?
Could I have had a heroic
princely life before you,
full of tumultuous
left-handed love?

Freedom

They can cancel every flight
as long as I get to watch you
read your brief.
They can run out of chicken
stuffed with shrimp if I
can slurp my soup with you
and sit through the worst
movies ever made with my
hand where it doesn't belong.
It's dark here, sweets,
no one will know, we're free.
Let them overcharge us for the dinner.
Let them lose our bags
and try to reroute us.
Where we are, we're airborne.

The Feast

Feast yourself on beauty
while you can, the useless
thing: the neck, the hip,
the road between the hills,
the short hairs on the chin,
the snow on the table.

Feast on silence,
nothing but the wind
moaning outside,
the shovel on the sidewalk,
feast on being here
in this bright room
while he is sleeping.

Tom in Rome

Bolder than Antonio Canova
outdoing the Apollo Belvedere,
you demolish every Red Guide reader's
half-baked callow notion of an
adequate response to what we see:
forensically investigating Daphne,
how she limb by limb becomes a tree,
you scant the art, stern sage who's always known
what matters in a figure is the stone.

You are toffee, you are sand in sunlight,
you are handsome, winsome, bright, and lithe:
chaste Carrara, blue-veined Parian,
hand-warmed Pentelic when you buck and writhe
more contorted than Laocoön,
diminutive fine subtle lordship, master-
work surpassing alabaster,
as I am tufa to your travertine.

Go ahead and shame us in the Forum
with your ironic fine decorum, do:
Antinous with glasses and umbrella,
deus ex machina of the novella
whose story was that my roads led to you.

Nomad,

bindle balanced on
your shoulder, with
Baby in his cage who
keeps on asking, "What
you want?" What do you
want, my bindle stiff:
your adolescent dream
of love for two, hot-
house dyad no one else
can enter, night cave
where you stare at the
TV devouring endless
lobsters on newspaper?
Your bed's in storage,
nomad, where will you
sleep? Where will you
find the sill to shelter
your impossible cymbi-
diums? Loner, gorgeous
lord of love in silence,
what will save you?

Madonna Enthroned with Saints

Lurid Piero lineup in my nightmare
flattened fixed
in the too-much light of Umbria

left: first love eighteen dark hair and glasses
    glistening sullen lip with bike and camera;

next: kneeling naked eyes rolled upward smirking
    no Sebastian no arrows just
    his attribute the bat he's leaning on;

right: the redhead stares unseeing pipe in pocket
    polo shirt and Levi's shouldering his bag of manuscripts;

and the nomad with birdcage and bindle
and that round unblemished open face;

and *center:* You! Bejeweled implacable
    enraged eyes flashing hopeless arms held out
    to demonstrate your angels mother of mercilessness
    (who lurks in the curtains by your chair?)

—while the hapless donor cowers half-size in the corner—

Why are you staring?

lineup of my failures
gone unlived untested choir of losses
judge mock me finger me my cavalcade
of beauties failed loves fallen loves
my fault my faulty loves my fallen loves!

Incantation

Pacing restless in
the waiting room
thrashing thresh-
ing on your thresh-
ing floor winnow-
ing assaying and
discarding seeking
finding cracks and
flaws and pouring
unrelenting love
into the cracked
flawed hourglass
that is always
emptying . . .

        How
to show you that
the bowl is brim-
ming these streets
the rooms your
heart has every-
thing . . . the body
that adored you is
the body the voice
that called your
name out is the
one there is no
water better than
the water that
travels unimpeded
down from Croton

fluoride-purified
and ever-ready to
flood your kitchen
sink at your com-
mand. Open the fau-
cet. Bend down.
Drink. Be healed.

Tinsel Tinsel

For M.C.

A fool for love, an inner refugee,
sees a peacock strutting in the birdhouse
high on a branch and fanning
the broadest, most articulate fan tail
the fool for love has ever seen.
"Come fly with me!" the fool calls to the peacock,
but the bright bird keeps strutting up and down
above the fool for love there on the ground.

A blackbird comes and settles on his shoulder.
His pecks are rough caresses as he asks him,
"Why do you keep staring at that tree?"
"Peacock!" the fool for love cries, but the blackbird
caws back, "Fool! Since when do peacocks fly?
Look around the birdhouse: see us towhees,
wrens and jays and blackbirds
flittering and swooping—
what we always do for free."

All the fool for love can do is stare.
His neck is permanently out of whack;
he doesn't care.
But one fine day in slanted light
he glances up as usual and spies
not his darling bird of paradise
but a hank of Christmas tinsel
trailing in the birdhouse breeze . . .

Even so he often murmurs,
"Peacock!" in his haunted dreams.
Ask me why, the reason's simple:
he's a fool for love, blackbirds
are blackbirds, peacocks peacocks,
tinsel tinsel.

Young Maple in Ghent

For R.F. and R.H.

In your yard this morning I can see
through the still summer air how every tree
(except the dead one on your neighbor's land)
stands exfoliated, spherical,
authoritative, magisterial,
replete the way that it was made to be
in the few long perfect days we get
before the drought and then the frost set in.

The younger maple rising on the hill
where it slopes to meet your neighbor's land,
is fledged by now and dense with chlorophyll,
and with luck will catch up with the others,
filling out its contours like its brothers,
rounding and adding rings as nature meant,
on your sloping, wind-washed hill in Ghent.

Ruins

for B.G.G.

A poem is a ruin. In Tulum
we got to know the Maya by their stones;
we saw the hole that held the royal bones
and a vegetable-dyed wall inside a room
displayed the crossed limbs of the Diving God
falling into sun-drenched blue-green water.
They were good like us at roads and slaughter
(though that they did without the wheel is odd).
As in the Sonnets, just the bones are there.
In the Sonnets, all there is, is bone:
trajectories and vectors, lines of stone
standing in for muscle, blood, and hair—
as someday, darling, stones and bones will be
all there is to stand for you and me.